To Larry

Lorraine Burkey

A Little Birdie Told Me

LORRAINE A. BURKEY

ARCHWAY
PUBLISHING

This is a work of fiction. All of the characters, names, incidents, organizations, and dialogue in this novel are either the products of the author's imagination or are used fictitiously.

Archway Publishing books may be ordered through booksellers or by contacting:

Archway Publishing
1663 Liberty Drive
Bloomington, IN 47403
www.archwaypublishing.com
844-669-3957

Because of the dynamic nature of the Internet, any web addresses or links contained in this book may have changed since publication and may no longer be valid. The views expressed in this work are solely those of the author and do not necessarily reflect the views of the publisher, and the publisher hereby disclaims any responsibility for them.

Any people depicted in stock imagery provided by Getty Images are models, and such images are being used for illustrative purposes only. Certain stock imagery © Getty Images.

ISBN: 978-1-6657-0090-0 (sc)
ISBN: 978-1-6657-0089-4 (hc)
ISBN: 978-1-6657-0091-7 (e)

Library of Congress Control Number: 2020925659

Print information available on the last page.

Archway Publishing rev. date: 02/04/2021

Contents

Acknowledgments

I am compelled to give God all the credit for the gift, inspiration, and creativity to develop these poems. Without him, there would be no book.

To my husband, Steven, who relentlessly pushed and prodded me to start the process of publishing these poems. His computer knowledge solved many of my concerns about presentation. Thank you from the bottom of my heart.

To family, friends, acquaintances, professionals, and all others, thank you for your opinions and encouragement that led to my decision to publish these poems.

Foreword

I have had the privilege of knowing Lorraine Burkey for a number of years. I have been fascinated by her positive life view, her grateful heart, and her ability to take life in stride. I am fully aware of her devastating stroke at such a young age, and how she came through this life-changing event with a warrior spirit and a zest for reaching out and living life to its fullest. Her poems reflect this adventure and simply resonate with anyone who reads her work. Lorraine is gifted with a way of writing a picture that clearly expresses thoughts and feelings most of us have been unable to do. Her work is an inspiration to anyone who loses sight of living life in the moment and has settled for a mediocre existence.

Bobbi J. Craigmyle, PsyD

My Way

It started out for me,
And mostly just for fun.
They help me sort my thoughts
As I change; I'm never done.

If something sounds familiar,
No doubt been said before.
I just had to say it my way.
It means just that much more.

So as I pause to share these
With whomever you may be,
You can be sure as life goes on
Many poems are yet to be.

No matter how you change
Or how far away you roam,
Maybe something in my words
Will bring their meaning home.

Introduction

Every one of us develops a dream of how life is going to be. As we grow and mature, that dream gets more detailed and refined. Careers, falling in love, family, children, and achievements are all parts of this dream. For the most part, these things become reality, give or take a few variations, but for others, this dream is totally erased from existence. For those, there is a challenge either to give in to a lost dream or find a way to make that dream come true from a whole new perspective. This book of poems portrays the former in such a way that whatever the age, stage of life, challenges, or perceived roadblocks are, one can take the steering wheel of life and realize that life is what you make it; the roads you take are your choice. These poems are about real life, real tragedies, real struggles, and real victories. They are a refreshment for the soul and a positive motivation to enjoy what is, not what could have been.

A Little Birdie Told Me

Where did these poems come from?
I really couldn't say.
A little birdie told me,
So I can remember it that way.

Preface

As a twenty-year-old, single, carefree girl, I had a good family. I had finished high school, was working a good job, and living on my own. What could get in the way of this? Without warning, I was struck down, totally down, by an atypical stroke that led the doctors to the conclusion that I would not likely survive, or at best I would be a vegetable. Of course I was unaware of any of this as I was in a coma for six weeks and in the hospital for four months.

When I first became conscious that I was alive, my first thoughts were of how different everything was. I knew my family and I knew something huge had happened to me, but I had a sense that I was about to begin a new and challenging life journey. My parents took me in for a long recovery, which was a tremendous blessing. Each day I became strong mentally about what happened to me and about how life was going to be for me now.

At the fullest of my recovery, I was left with partial vision in both eyes and partial paralysis of my left side. Most everything I had done before had to be relearned using only one side of my body. In addition, my brain had to reroute neuronal connections to different parts of my brain as I could not reason and perform mental functions in the same way I did before. As daunting a task as this was, I did not let it take control of my will to achieve an independent and productive life.

This complete turnabout at the age of twenty is the springboard of my poetic creativity that puts words into emotional understanding of life. Some of my poems were written for special occasions, like holidays and birthdays. The largest portion of my poems were thoughts that started out with words that rhymed. The thoughts would not leave me alone until I wrote them down. Then I could get back to what I had been doing. When each poem was finished, I then marveled as to how I managed to write it that way.

I would not change anything about my life. It has made me who I am, which is far more wonderful than any dream a twenty-year-old girl could have about her future life.

1

An Invitation to Your Heart

Fairytale Frogs

Love stories are for romantics
Who believe in fairytales.
That's just fine and dandy,
Till you go to hook up with males.

I've had my share of frogs,
But nothing happened there.
So I guess I gave up looking,
And life was empty air.

One more frog came hopping by,
And luckily it was you.
Fairy tales may be a joke,
But dreams still do come true.

Happily ever after
Is expecting quite a lot.
Our love is something special,
And we're giving it all we've got.

At Peace

You have to know it took a while
To become a brand-new me,
A couple of years down the road
To like who I would be.

I can't say I was thrilled
To go through every stage,
Constantly relearning
As I lived it page by page.

I can't say life is easy
As I live each fold and crease.
But I wouldn't trade it anyway;
I'm living life at peace.

Sorry

I'm sorry I hurt you.
That wasn't cool.
I'm sorry I made you
Feel like a fool.

If it happens for a reason,
I still feel the guilt.
The bruises I feel
Push the walls that I've built.

I'm sorry I hurt you.
I thought I was strong.
I'm sorry I hurt you
Because I was wrong.

Tell Me Your Story

Tell me your story.
Don't tell me a lie.
How did you reach
For your piece of the pie?

Did you do it with kindness?
Did you do it right?
Did the goal that you reached
Make it worth the fight?

When you look in a mirror,
What do you see?
We know when you get there
It wasn't for free.

The smile from your heart,
So warm and sincere,
Gives me hope that somehow
I can get there from here.

The kindness you've shown
In whatever you do
Makes me glad that my life
Put you in there too.

The Guy

Of course we love duct tape;
It fixes everything.
When all is said and done,
We feel like a king.

Who needs to call the guy
When we need to fill that hole?
I can be the guy,
Just hand me another roll.

9

Life at Large

A Brand-New Road

Where did you come from?
How could I know
That you would show up
And my life would glow?

I didn't expect
What life has bestowed,
The warmth of life
On a brand-new road.

A Caring Hurt

Don't let my heart turn cold
Just because it hurts today.
Don't let me shrug my shoulder
Because the world thinks it's okay.

My heart is having growing pains
For having learned to care,
But it can keep on hurting.
It's making room for you in there.

A Dream Remembered

I heard a song from yesterday
That almost brought a tear,
And though it brought no memory,
I almost felt one near.

I searched my heart and mind
For what the song had stirred.
But I came up quite empty,
Just some dreams that time had blurred.

So why do I feel so strange
Hearing a song from my past?
Am I grieving for my dreams
That somehow didn't last?

Today is so very different
From what I thought it'd be.
I was so busy growing up
I forgot the child in me.

It's hard to say goodbye
To dreams that won't come true.
My heart is playing catch-up
To what my mind already knew.

So play those special songs,
And that way I can tell
That deep inside of me
The child is still alive and well.

A Heart's Smile

I want your heart to smile
With warmth and laughter too.
One that you will keep
Through whatever you do.

May love wrap its arms around you
To keep you warm inside.
May you embrace the happiness
Of a heart that opens wide.

About Me

When did I start
Not wanting to feel?
When did I shrug
Like life's no big deal?

I want to smile;
I need to see that
There is more to life.
It's not all about me.

Always Have You There

I was supposed to be in love with you;
I really thought I was.
But the heart gets very tricky.
Now I know it does.

The scars I gave to you
But put the blame on me.
Things happen for a reason.
You are the person meant to be.

Those scars I carry too.
You really did care.
So the person that I am
Will always have you there.

Always Living

All I really know,
Wherever I got my start,
Is that I will always be living
From the bottom of my heart.

Always Time

Life is short,
Or so they say.
But when I was young,
It didn't seem that way.

There's always tomorrow
For dreams we held high.
Always time
For our piece of the pie.

The time we had
As memories replay,
They bring a smile
For back in the day.

Another Point of View

So heavy is my heart
To hear the news,
With all the bitter
And negative views.

There's a light at the end of the tunnel
With another point of view,
Someone who keeps the faith
That we love each other too.

Around the Bend

In the spring of '74,
I was only twenty.
Life seemed to have a lot in store,
And I was offered plenty.

But something upstairs broke inside.[1]
I almost was no more.
And though it wasn't likely,
I made it through the door.

Every day I'm determined
To start the day anew.
There's sunshine in my heart
With a sunny point of view.

Nobody promised it would be easy.
There's a challenge in what I do.
The love of Mom and Dad
Was there to see me through.

There was a time when I thought
My world had come to an end,
But time has proven to me
That I'm just traveling 'round the bend.

---

[1] Arteriovenous malformation (AVM).

Be Kind

I'm not any
Better than you.
I have hurts
And worries too.

I know I'm blessed,
Without a doubt,
But my heart hurts
If you shut me out.

Please be kind
In all you do.
Please understand
I need love too.

Because of You

You're never too little.
Though you'll never know
How something you did
Changed the status quo.

When your heart is good
You feel good too.
The future is changed
Because of you.

Better

It happened for a reason.
Let the future unfold.
We play it by ear.
We can't put it on hold.

But as I play it back,
Right down to the letter,
No matter what the reason,
I wish that I'd been better.

Better Today

I was wrong—simple as that.
But I can't change it now.
If it happened for a reason,
What would I change and how?

I still feel guilty
For being that way,
But I vow to myself
That I will be better today.

Break Down My Walls

I have a special face
That I wear for public view
To hide me from myself
And especially from you.

Sometimes when we're close
And I feel you really care,
I almost let you in,
But somehow I never dare.

I'm afraid you'll laugh at me
With a smirk you cannot hide.
So I pretend I'm hard,
Never showing my softer side.

I feel like no one knows
The person who is me.
Instead of being so phony,
I'd like to live spontaneously.

If I just knew you wouldn't laugh
And you'd love me anyway,
I'd give up this phony game
And not care what people say.

But the walls I've built around me
Make it difficult to do.
Please be so very patient.
All my hope depends on you.

So if it's any comfort,
When all is said and done,
We all feel this way—
Each and every one.

Bully Me

You may not understand me—
And I can't make you see—
But you do not have the right
To change or bully me.

Even if I'm wrong
As you raise your voice,
If I'm not hurting you,
It's my right to make that choice.

Burning Bridges

When is life going to get better?
Or will it stay the same?
There is no more excitement.
Do I have to play this game?

Somewhere up ahead,
There has to be a bend.
This lonely stretch of highway
Cannot be without an end.

If I quit now, I'll never know
Just what lies ahead.
So I keep pretending
Today's a chapter I haven't read.

Maybe there's a turn
Over the next hill,
A field for me to harvest,
Something interesting to till.

Yup, I was right.
Here, finally, is my turn.
And now I have to ask myself,
What bridges do I want to burn?

Changing Goals

Been wishing things were different
And that problems would go away,
That life would just ease up
And let things go my way.

I feel like a failure,
With the pieces out of place.
Maybe it wasn't meant to be
That I'd fit in with the human race.

But God doesn't make junk,
So maybe I've been blind.
If I can't have just what I want,
I'll just have to change my mind.

Choose

Real life happens.
You have a choice.
What you choose
Becomes your voice.

You can whine
About what's not fair,
Or you can choose
To show you care.

You can be sure
Someone's watching you,
Learning from all
The things you do.

If you feel love,
They will too.
Rest assured
They're glad you're you.

Choose Peace

We all feel lonely
When we hurt inside.
We all feel good
When the sun opens wide.

I live a miracle
That brings me peace.
One I hope and pray
Will never cease.

The sun comes out
And sits awhile.
So I choose peace;
It makes me smile.

Compare

If you look at the good,
You don't suffer the past.
You'll find your future,
The one that will last.

There will never be another you;
You really are that rare.
Life gets so much better
When you learn not to compare.

COVID-19

This time of quarantine
Brought it home to me,
Just how comfortable it is
Just to be me.

It saddens my heart
What all is lost.
We're all in this together,
No matter what it costs.

I promise I'll be kind
Just because you're you.
The group hug that we have
Will be loving quite a few.

Decorations of My Heart

The moments of my life
Decorate my heart,
And there's nothing I can do
That would change any part.

Some of them make me sad.
Some make me a little proud.
Some will bring a tear.
Others make me laugh out loud.

As days go by I realize
A memory lane will start,
And my arms will wrap around
The decorations of my heart.

Denial

You'll never know how much it hurt
When I broke up with you.
Something took hold of my heart
And squeezed it black and blue.

Oh, I was in denial.
I was perfectly okay.
There was a hollow feeling
As I turned and walked away.

That feeling of denial
Echoes with me still.
And though it's in the past,
I know it always will.

Do What's Right

I'm tired of politics—
Tired of the sham,
Tired of the posturing
For Uncle Sam.

What happened to serving
For the common good,
For improving our country
As they know they should?

They're lining their pockets
For personal greed
Instead of providing
What we desperately need.

Come on, stand up
And join the fight!
Look in the mirror
And do what's right.

Does It Really Matter?

Does it really matter
What we do with all our days?
And what difference does it make
If we never mend our ways?

But someone's always watching
The little things you do.
You never know when something great
Was subtly inspired by you.

So maybe today is boring
And exasperating too.
But I will do my best
To set an example for you.

And if there comes a day
When my row's too hard to hoe,
I hope you'll tell me I have helped
In ways I'll never know.

Enough

If I told you my story
You'd laugh, maybe cry.
I can't explain,
And I don't know why.

So many days
Filled with stuff.
I was supposed to be here,
And that is enough.

Every Life's a Winner

If I had been the firstborn,
I might feel more like leading.
And if there hadn't been a war,
Our hearts would not be bleeding.

But playing with all the ifs
And looking for things to blame
Don't help me with today
Nor help me understand the game.

Looking on the bright side
Isn't really being dumb.
It's better than the other side,
Expecting the worst to come.

I can wallow in self-pity
For the things that life has done.
But I know deep in my heart,
I'm responsible for number one.

If I walk the streets alone,
There's a chance of being mugged.
If I run for public office,
My phones might end up bugged.

There's something to be said
For taking life by the horns.
You might end up with roses,
Or you might end up with thorns.

Every life has meaning,
And we all pay our dues.
You are the author of your life.
It's up to you to choose.

Every Ripple

I'm just an average Joe,
Living day to day.
Not expecting much,
Just hoping to find my way.

What difference does it make?
There's nothing special that I do.
I live, I laugh, I love,
But does it matter to you?

You may not understand,
Though everyone should,
That everything we do
Needs to be something good.

Every ripple goes on forever,
Although we never really see,
That everything you've done before
Is creating what we see.

I hope by now you know
How important you are
As everything you've done
Has already traveled far.

I don't want to hear
You're just an average Joe,
You have changed the world.
More than you know.

You really do matter.
You need to see
You are important.
You were meant to be.

Everyday Heroes

My heroes have always been people,
The kind you meet every day.
They go about their lives
And lend you a hand on their way.

They have a sense of country
And doing what is right.
If you're one of the down and out,
They help you see the light.

Maybe there was a time
When they needed to be shown.
If they see you have no smile,
They give you one of their own.

So if you're on the street
And a smile comes your way,
Just think of them as a hero,
The kind you meet every day.

Everyone

Did you think I didn't notice
All the good things that you do?
So many acts of kindness
For more than just a few.

Thank you is not enough;
We need to pass it on.
The warmth and love we share
Includes each and everyone.

Filling Empty Spaces

I feel so very strange
When someone I know has died.
Something has gone away,
And my world is not as wide.

Then it starts me thinking
Life is a complicated weave.
And the people I hold dear
Will someday take their leave.

So I try to imagine
When each person goes away,
I find myself just blinking
To hold the tears at bay.

I know life will go on
In spite of my state of mind.
God, help me find a way
To fill the space they leave behind.

Friendship

Life hasn't been so easy,
But really not that hard.
Sometimes it makes me laugh,
Like a funny birthday card.

It's only when I'm lonely
And feeling sort of blue,
I think of what I'm missing
And want a life that's new.

But then I think of you.
How much your friendship means to me,
And if I wasn't who I am,
Our friendship might never be.

And so I wrote this poem
And hope that you will see
Whether we laugh, whether we cry,
You mean a lot to me.

Going On

Yes I get depressed.
I just keep going on.
I cannot believe
Everything good is gone.

Nobody promised me
Life was only good.
I was really hoping
Somehow that it would.

We don't know tomorrow
What dues we have to pay.
I just keep the faith
I'll keep going anyway.

Happy Endings

I believe in happy endings,
Though no one's promised me.
I believe in hugs and kisses
And the comfort tears can be.

If self-esteem is love,
Then whatever life will be,
I'll have a happy ending
Because I have promised me.

Have a Purpose

Did it surprise you
With what I didn't say?
Did you think it didn't matter
As you went along your way?

Some part of who I am
Attached itself to you.
Somehow along the way,
It changed what you would do.

We all have a purpose,
Though we may never see,
What we said and did
Became part of history.

Heart and Home

This house has been our refuge,
Our haven through the years.
It's heard the laughter, felt the love,
And watched us dry our tears.

And though the walls are drafty,
The plaster cracked in places too,
This home is filled with love;
The memories number quite a few.

A part of me feels sad
To leave this house behind.
This home that was our castle,
The only one of its kind.

But home is where the heart is,
And it's time for someplace new.
We'll take the memories with us
Because our hearts are moving too.

Here Together

We are all here together,
The big and the small.
Everybody counts,
The short and the tall.

No one can be forgotten,
No matter who we are.
Everything we do
Travels near and far.

We cannot shrug our shoulders
And say, "Oh, well, whatever."
Everyone starts a ripple,
And it will go on forever.

How Do You Know?

You don't understand
What I was thinking,
To be so cavalier
Without even blinking.

It doesn't make sense,
So dumb and absurd,
Without looking back
And not saying a word.

So who are you
To judge what you see
When what happened to you
Did not happen to me?

So how do you know
What I should do
When what happened to me
Did not happen to you?

How Much I Care

I love you so.
My heart just smiles.
It keeps expanding
For miles and miles.

I want you to know
How much I care.
Everything sparkles
When you are there.

How Special You Are

I wonder if you know
How special you are.
I wonder if you know
You're someone's wish upon a star.

Someone needed you
To be here today.
They needed you to change things
In your special kind of way.

You have changed the world
Everywhere you go.
You are so very special,
And I hope by now you know.

Humanity Allowed

Thinking back is fairly safe
Because you set yourself aside.
And things you couldn't see before
Have lost their places to hide.

It's hard to understand
How we're feeling as we grow.
And see exactly who we are,
So we hurry to and fro.

Sometimes it's hard to forgive yourself
For things you did back then.
But you still feel the guilt
For what happened way back when.

So be your own best friend,
And yes, you can be proud.
None of us is perfect.
Rest assured that you're allowed.

I Didn't Know

Things didn't turn out
Like I thought they would.
But I kept trying
And hoping they would.

It pushed me one way.
I turned it around.
I was very persistent
And stood my ground.

I like where I'm at.
It made me grow.
Now I'm so glad
I didn't know.

I Don't Have to Guess

You'd ask me a question,
And I gave it my best.
I was satisfied,
Though it was just a guess.

Time passes by,
And with it we grow.
I don't have to guess.
I say, "Gee, I just don't know."

I Just Pray

When we are up,
Ain't life grand?
When we are down,
We don't understand.

When good things happen,
We take it in stride.
When bad things happen,
We want to hide.

Searching for answers
Can lead us astray.
I may never know,
So I just pray.

As life goes on,
We keep complaining.
We hope for the best
And keep on praying.

If My Teddy Bear Could Talk

If my teddy bear could talk,
I know just what he'd say:
"I care and love you, too,
In my own fuzzy kind of way."

We would cry together
As we snuggle side by side.
A place where we'd find comfort
While our hearts are open wide.

I'm glad he's always there
To keep me company.
He'll never move away,
And we will always be.

No matter what my hurts are,
Or what happens along the way,
I know that Teddy loves me
In his fuzzy kind of way.

Into Me

I have a story I want to tell.
I know you have one too.
It colors everything we think,
And a message will come through.

I want to hear the story
Of how you came to be,
So what you are sharing
Will be woven into me.

It Doesn't Really Matter

I have a special secret
That I want to share with you.
Something that helps me every day,
Though I didn't realize I knew.

Life can drive you crazy
With the things that can go wrong.
Sometimes it just gets out of hand,
And I feel I'm not that strong.

I can't seem to find the answer.
And as time goes, I get madder.
But if I try to think it through,
I find it doesn't really matter.

With all life's little things,
It's really hard to tell.
If it doesn't really matter,
I can shrug and say, "Oh, well."

So decide what is important
In a world of mindless chatter.
You'll know when you can shrug and say,
"Oh, well, it doesn't matter."

I've Won

After ten steps forward,
It's now six steps back.
Arthritis is here
Like a sneak attack.

I'm older now,
So it's harder too.
I keep on going
Because that's what I do.

I look for answers.
When all is done,
The sun will shine,
And I know I've won.

Just Be You

Don't be too strong.
Don't be too soft.
Don't hold your feelings
Too highly aloft.

We all keep hoping—
We really do try—
Without understanding
Or knowing why.

Looking back,
We hope to see
The person we really
Wanted to be.

More often than not
What we really see
Is how that person
Could turn out to be me.

As life goes on,
What can you do?
Don't overthink it,
Just be you.

Just Relax

Guardian of my heart,
Can't you just relax?
Caution is fine,
But so is living to the max.

Take a chance.
Let it go.
Or what you missed
You will never know.

You may get hurt,
And you could fall.
Just take a chance.
Give it your all.

Just Take Note

My heart hurts,
But that's okay.
I'll keep on loving
Anyway.

Maybe I wonder
Why I'm alive.
But just take note,
I will survive.

Just the Way It Is

It's hard to explain.
Why should I try?
But I see that look
You want me to justify.

It's very annoying
As it's none of your biz.
I'll be offhand.
That's the way that it is.

Keep Going

There was a time when I thought
My world had come to an end.
But time has proven to me
That I'm traveling around the bend.

Keep on Going

Growing old was always someday,
Never really now.
All of a sudden, here it is.
Exactly what do I do and how?

From a distance I always knew
How it was supposed to be.
Well all bets are off
Now that it's happening to me.

The life I live right now
Comes from seeds that I've been sewing.
And now that I've grown old,
I pray and keep on going.

Kind Words

What did you say?
What was that word?
I can hardly believe
That it's what I heard.

Did you know that it hurt,
And it sticks in my mind
That the words you use
Are not the thoughtful kind?

I try to be kind
In all that I say.
And I hope in return
You will treat me that way.

Kindness

There's a place inside your heart
Where comfort and love reside.
A place that knows your story
With conscience as your guide.

I hope that there is kindness
In the smile you wear today.
Where we all share a home
As we're living day by day.

Legacy of Love

I want to be there for you,
To kiss the hurts away.
I want to share the good times
And be there day by day.

The times that make us cry
Will be hard for us to share.
But it will create a special bond
For the way we truly care.

There will be disappointments
Sometimes along the way.
But knowing we love each other
Softens the price there is to pay.

I know it won't be perfect,
But we'll have something rare.
A haven in each other's arms,
And we'll find contentment there.

There will be peace inside my heart
That comes from loving you.
Thank you, dear, for loving me.
You make my life brand new.

Lesson of Life

It took a major crisis
To turn my life around,
To make me realize
A better world could be found.

I've learned life isn't fair,
But that doesn't bother me.
I'm having a grand old time
Discovering how unique my life can be.

Don't think I have no questions
For I'm still learning yet.
Life has taught me many things,
None of which I will forget.

The price I paid was very high.
This lesson might be done.
But just what makes me think
I can get through life on only one?

Life in America

Listening to the news,
It's hard to understand.
We all seem to think
We deserve a helping hand.

We're so used to having everything
Our little hearts' desires.
The end justifies the means,
So what if we turn liars.

What does it mean to do without?
Why should we sacrifice?
We want our cake and eat it too,
And never pay the price.

Now the government's going broke.
We finally reached the limit.
Someone is causing a ruckus
However we try to trim it.

So easy was the coasting
Down that stretch of road.
Now that it's turned uphill,
It's time we carried the load.

Still I believe in people,
Though it seems we've lost our way.
I know I'll always be proud
To be part of the USA.

Life Is a Song

Life is a song.
Life is a dance.
Life is a kick.
Just give it a chance.

We never know
Just what it will bring.
So when it happens,
Just let your heart sing.

Life Isn't Fair

While I was growing up,
I was told life wasn't fair.
And naïve as I had been,
I thought it must be rare.

But people do mean things,
And you have to sort it out.
I've been dealt my share,
And I no longer doubt.

I had to realize
You can't retaliate in kind.
If there really was an eye for an eye,
The whole world would be blind.

Life's Shoes

Nobody knows what you've been through.
Nobody's walked in your shoe.
They may try to empathize,
But that's all they really do.

The color of our choices
Relate to way back when
The pain of how it was
Comes back again and again.

We all have pity parties
For what we couldn't see.
But happiness came calling
For those who chose plan B.

I didn't see it coming;
No one gave me a key.
But as I look ahead,
I like this brand-new me.

Looking Back

I go forward,
Yet I look back,
Putting all my regrets
In a heavy sack.

I can't change the past,
Only tomorrow.
Why do I pass judgment
With longing sorrow?

So what lies ahead
And what I will be,
It will be good.
I have promised me.

Looking for Happiness

It's so easy to get depressed,
Especially when you're lonely.
You start reliving your life
And mourning each, "If only …"

Sometimes we can control
Just how our life will be.
But more often it turns out
The road is longer than we can see.

No matter how much you have,
Somehow it should be better.
You want it to be perfect,
Right down to the letter.

When it comes to being happy,
The answer we can't find.
But no matter how much you agonize,
It's only a state of mind.

Looking for Mr. Perfect

I wrote a poem about you,
But I think it's only fair to say
That while I put the blame on you,
Somehow it didn't happen that way.

I said you were thoughtless and selfish.
But I had my moments too.
So I had to write this poem
To set myself straight about you.

We were always attracted to each other.
I guess we drove ourselves crazy
Making each other jealous.
Could we really have been that lazy?

Neither of us would sacrifice
A molecule of our pride.
Maybe if we hadn't been so foolish,
We could have skipped that silly ride.

I wonder how it would be
If ever I saw you again.
Would I still be the same,
Expecting a perfect ten?

Love Lost

So callous, so careless.
What did I do?
It wasn't love,
Just happy with you.

So heavy my heart,
I didn't know why.
With guilty resolve,
I just said goodbye.

Love Flows

Wrap your love around me
To comfort my lonely heart.
Keep me safe and warm
For this time that we're apart.

And I will do the same for you.
I'll be there deep inside
To warm you from the inside out,
So your heart won't have to hide.

If we can keep it going,
Back and forth and roundabout,
Our love will flow together
With no way to sort it out.

After a while we'll realize
We've really truly won.
The love will be like our ring
As we've become as one.

Love Happens

What is this word called "love"?
Why does it scare us so?
We're reaching and wanting
Because we never know.

Love you cannot see,
Maybe were not aware.
Love only happens
When we know how much we care.

Love Is Kind

For all the hurts you've given me,
I'm hoping to forgive
So I can give myself
The life I want to live.

I believe in love;
It's a caring state of mind.
I believe in love.
I believe in being kind.

Love You So

Where did you come from?
I'm so glad you're here.
You give me a life
Whenever you're near.

You kick-start my life.
You make it flow.
You tickle my heart.
And I love you so.

Making Love

Sometimes in your eyes
I can see the little boy,
The one who was so sick
When someone took away his toy.

I've seen you when you're mad
And things aren't going right.
I've watched you do your share
When it came time to fight.

I know that spark of anger
That jumps out from your eyes.
And it's not hard to tell
Someone's been telling lies.

And yet there are times they sparkle
When you give that special smile.
How well I know that look.
I know it's just your style.

You made my heart so happy
That day we flew our kite.
You warmed my very soul
As we walked late that night.

And when I see our kite
So free and high above,
Some call it having fun,
I like to call it making love.

Missed It

The odds of finding you
I couldn't calculate.
So when you came along,
I was thinking it must be fate.

For over twenty years
We gave it our best shot.
We laughed and cried and grumbled,
And even fought a lot.

Things have settled down,
And I'm still in love with you.
Thanks for hanging in there
Like we always do.

So when you are upset,
With our favorite insults hurled,
I just want you to know
I wouldn't have missed it for the world.

More Than One Me

Of all the poems I've written,
Not one of them is me.
You'd have to read them all
To come close to who I'd be.

For no one is ever stagnant,
Always staying the same.
We each are many people,
All under just one name.

And someday if I discover
That I only have one side,
I'll know because I stay the same.
Somewhere my soul has died.

My Choice

We all have boundaries—
At least we should.
Don't tell me what to do
As it's for my own good.

With life and liberty,
I have a voice.
I'll do it my way.
I have that choice.

My Color

I chose my color
At an early age.
Life goes on
Page by page.

Some pages are sad
And tragic too.
Some pages are torn.
So what did I do?

I'm looking at pages
For quite a while.
I'm so glad that my color
Is hope and a smile.

My Forever

I wanted to write a song
Warm and sweet and clever.
But all I want to say
Is you are my forever.

My Home Is You

If words could describe the feeling
Of having you with me,
Then they'd be soft and warm,
Full of peaceful serenity.

They'd tell of the lonesome ache
Whenever you're away.
And sing a joyful song
For the rainbow in my day.

But most of all would be
The symphony of sighs
To express how I've come home
When I look into your eyes.

My Own Boat

I've been playing Pollyanna
Without negativity.
I've been looking both ways
With my own integrity.

I'm rowing my own boat.
I believe in where I'm going.
I never give up;
I just keep on rowing.

My Song

Life isn't fair.
I know that it's true.
But when it actually happens,
What will I do?

Will I be angry
And ask, "Why me?"
When I look in the mirror,
Will I like what I see?

As time goes on,
I hope I'm strong
And that my life story
Becomes my song.

My Sparkler

I didn't believe in you,
But you found me anyway.
If I'm really crazy,
What could I possibly say?

Real love doesn't happen fast;
It takes time to be real.
How do I know that love
Is really what I feel?

I took a leap of faith.
I was hoping from the start.
I'm so glad you found me.
You are the sparkle in my heart.

My Special Style

What is this life I'm living?
What's it all about?
Am I living it the right way?
Maybe I chose the wrong route.

I realize I'm different
And yet quite normal too.
I guess I have no business
Comparing my life to you.

I like the way I'm living;
It's my own special style.
But I wonder what it would be like
To try yours for a while.

Some folks want to be different;
They enjoy the controversial.
But life should be so much more
Than an empty Pepsi commercial.

My Style

It's just not my style
To complain of what's not fair.
I just look forward
To know it's everywhere.

Being negative
Is not my way at all.
I am happy being me,
A choice that's mine to call.

I can see the sadness,
And it hurts to see you cry.
I don't have the answers
When you turn and ask me why.

I want to see the happy
And only hope for good.
No, life isn't fair,
And that's just understood.

My Valentine

My funny valentine
Is the sunshine of my life.
And telling you just how I feel
Should be easy for a wife.

How do I say you're wonderful
And make it still ring true?
I find I'm using worn-out words,
While hoping they'll sound new.

So honey, here's to you,
My message from the heart.
Thank you for the warmest love
That grows from a humble start.

Not so Simple

Starting out I knew it all;
The answers were so clear.
And anyone who thought otherwise,
I just didn't have time to hear.

And for a time things went well.
It seemed I had been right.
Life was so bright and easy;
All my goals were in my sight.

So it came as quite a shock
When life led me quite astray.
And the answers that I thought were black and white
Have proved to have more gray.

On Probation

I love you, dear.
You know I do.
So when we fight,
I feel so blue.

Our laughter fills the house.
Although there is frustration,
That's when I want to tell you
This love is on probation.

Only One You

Everyone is special.
I can see it in your eyes.
Life is to be lived
Wearing no disguise.

Wherever you are living
Or whatever you do,
You have to realize
There's only one you.

Our Flag

So much courage,
So much heart.
Our country was born
From a humble start.

The bombs and rockets
Were everywhere.
But when they turned to look,
The flag was still there.

There's a catch in my heart;
That's how much I care.
When they turned to look,
The flag was still there.

Outside the Box

To all the people
From back in the day,
Life got complicated
As we found our way.

We just didn't know
What would knock off our socks.
Real life happens
Outside the box.

Over Again

One day at a time
Is so easy to say.
Worry just happens
Along the way.

Sometimes in the morning,
With my coffee cup,
I'm determined to win,
And I'll never give up.

The angst of it all
Way back when,
Please don't ask me
To do it again.

Over the Hill

It's finally official:
You're now over the hill.
And though I asked the pharmacist,
He couldn't recommend a pill.

So I hunted through the store
To see what I could find,
Though it's hard to keep up with your wife;
I hope you're not too far behind.

I decided on some BENGAY
To keep your muscles warm.
So when your wife gets frisky,
It won't do your body harm.

I spotted some Grecian Formula
To retain your youthful hair.
So when you and I are walking,
We'll still make a striking pair.

You'll never have to share,
So you keep it in the house.
No one else will need it,
Most definitely not your spouse.

I just can't find the words.
It must be hard to be so old.
But we'll hide it as long as we can
With all the products to be sold.

I promise we'll be careful
When walking in the rain.
And tomorrow, if need be,
We'll go shopping for a cane.

Part of Me

Nobody promised me,
But look at what I've got.
Not something you can see,
But I know it's quite a lot.

I know not to compare,
Though it's hard for you to see
That love and peace and joy
Are all a part of me.

Pieces of You

I might not really know you,
But you've touched me anyway.
Just by passing through my life,
You've helped to guide my way.

If I add you all together,
There's a hint of who is me.
But life is more than simple math,
More like geometry.

Where one will take away,
Another one will give.
So I evolve in pieces
With each day I have to live.

Some people seem to be alike
But are actually multiplied.
And just to keep the balance,
Some of you divide.

But we're not just lumped together;
Each one is unique.
And what I get from you
Is a special part I seek.

If there's someone in my life
I think I should delete,
But now it's just too late;
I wouldn't be complete.

So life is like a jigsaw,
But the pieces always stay.
Even those you didn't like
Will never go away.

Be careful with the pieces
To be sure they really fit.
As they will make up who you are
Bit by little bit.

Playing Solitaire

I've gotten very good
At playing solitaire
And being my own best friend
When no one else is there.

The TV keeps me company
When friends forget to call.
There are roomies, friends, and family
To keep me off the wall.

But then you come along
And wake me from my game.
You give me love and romance,
And nothing's been the same.

So now you've gone away,
And I know that you don't care.
I wish you'd never come.
I was good at solitaire.

Please Don't Ask

I've been hurt before,
Though you can't see the scars.
You'd think that I'd give up
And quit wishing on a star.

But nothing will keep me down.
I know that I'm worthwhile,
And though it takes some time,
I bounce back with a smile.

If you would go away,
I'd know just what to do.
And though I know that I'd survive,
Please don't ask me to.

Private Lives, Private Choices

I thought I'd heard it all
And life had made me strong.
But living life day by day
Has somehow proved me wrong.

There's no way for you to know
When someone will come your way
And try to run your life.
They just want to have their say.

There's no way I can explain
All the things that I've been through.
I have a private side;
I don't owe that much to you.

Sometimes you'll disagree
And maybe even scoff.
Though I try to be polite,
I'll just tell you to buzz off.

Maybe you think you're helping,
But it's up to me to choose.
No thanks, I'll do it my way.
You're not walking in my shoes.

Pulling for You

I sing your joy,
I cry your pain,
Something my heart
Just can't explain.

In the quiet,
When you're all alone,
You contemplate
Your personal zone.

If you're afraid
And timid, too,
I want to wrap
My arms around you.

I hope you find
Your personal song.
I've been pulling for you
All along.

Puppy's Loving Eyes

Our dog looks back at us
With a puppy's loving eyes.
They're always waiting for us
In spite of our goodbyes.

If ever they incur our wrath,
They love us anyway.
They come back hoping for love
No matter what we say.

Their greeting bowls us over
Whenever we've been gone.
And though he knows we'll do it again,
He thinks that he has won.

Although we don't deserve it,
It always will be.
Those puppy-dog eyes
Will be there loving me.

Reaching Out

My heart just aches.
I don't know why.
I feel your pain,
And I want to cry.

You don't know me,
But that's okay.
I just care.
I'm made that way.

We all need
Someone to care.
I want to be
The one who's there.

It warms my heart
Without a doubt.
I really care.
I'm reaching out.

Regrets

A memory sneaks in,
One that I regret.
I don't want to remember;
I'd rather forget.

I should've been better.
Even back in the day,
That just wasn't cool
To be acting that way.

I can't change it now.
It happened back then.
I vow to be better.
It won't happen again.

Remember Today

I've wasted so much time
Regretting yesterday,
Wanting to forget.
But it bugs me anyway.

While trying to forget,
There's not much I can say.
I need to live my life
So I can remember today.

Remember When

I remember
The good ole days
Through rose-colored glasses
And a distant haze.

I remember the good times
And some of the bad.
The moments of heartache,
And the dreams I had.

Today's not exactly
What I had in mind,
With so many struggles
Of the worrying kind.

Live for the moment.
Live for today.
Or those rose-colored glasses
Will take it away.

Look at today
And what it has been
As it will become
Your, "Remember when."

Repeatedly

How do I explain
What it is you cannot see,
The many bruising hurts
That shred my heart repeatedly?

Quietly my soul
I've been rocking to and fro,
Giving it love
For things I didn't know.

There's a flower in my heart
That will forever be,
And I want you to know
It will bloom repeatedly.

Right Now

Did you know
I was there once, too,
Making mistakes,
And more than just a few?

So young and foolish—
And selfish too—
I just kept going,
Hoping for something new.

If I could erase,
Though I don't know how,
I would have to give up
Who I am right now.

Rocking My Heart

What is this little ache
When I hear a lonely song,
This melancholy tune
That makes my heart just sing along?

I can't say I'm sad,
Though I'm feeling somewhat bruised.
Something touched my heart,
And I'm sitting here confused.

In the days ahead,
With the memories I keep,
Somehow along the way
I'll be rocking my heart to sleep.

Seasons

I'm so sick of winter,
The wind chill, and the snow.
I'm homesick for a heatwave
Instead of twenty-five below.

I'd like to hear the birds
And the melody each sings.
I'd like to feel the sunshine
And the greenery it brings.

Next fall I'll be tired
Of humidity and heat
And look forward to bulky clothes
And the cozy fireside seat.

I guess I wouldn't like it
If it always stayed the same.
But especially at winter's end
I'm sick of the winter game.

I'll sure enjoy the summer,
With all the pleasures I can find.
Winter will come again.
I just hope it will be kind.

Sing to Me

Sing me a song
That makes love to me.
Make it soft.
Sing it lovingly.

A song that wraps around me
If only for a while.
A song that warms my heart
And leaves a secret smile.

Take a Chance

I have money in the bank,
So I'm prepared
In case something happens
And I get scared.

The husband really
Likes to spend
Like there's no tomorrow
And there will be no end.

Here I am,
Taking a chance.
We meet in the middle,
And then we dance.

The Long Goodbye

Dad, it breaks my heart
You don't know me anymore.
I'm sorry you had to see
That slowly fading door.

And if it's any comfort,
As this just keeps on growing,
We hope you take a step
And then you keep on going.

The Love We Share

I love how much we laugh
And being silly too.
The way you hold my hand
Is part of loving you.

You put the sparkle in my eyes
And the glow inside my heart.
The special things we say,
The glue that cannot be pulled apart.

When love expands our hearts,
I cannot explain how much I care.
The peace of loving you
Will always be there.

From the bottom of my heart
All I really know
As the years go by is
This love will always grow.

This love that we share
Feels so very grand.
As you reach for mine,
I'll be giving you my hand.

The Mirror

I've looked in the mirror.
Just what can I say?
I've started to talk
About back in the day.

The things we thought
Would never be
Are somehow there
For all to see.

We roll with the punches,
Or at least we try.
We laugh and play
And sometimes cry.

I looked in the mirror;
I like what I see.
I wouldn't go back.
I like being me.

When I kick back
And think awhile,
The laughs and loves
They make me smile.

The Seeds You Plant

Yesterday was rainy
For all the things I couldn't do.
Today is partly cloudy,
And the sun is breaking through.

Yes, I took my time
In healing all my wounds
And all the winters of my life.
Help me cherish more the Junes.

It's hard to understand
Exactly what the fuss is.
You dwell on what is wrong with life;
I'm working on the plusses.

Okay, it isn't perfect,
But I take it day by day.
And everything I say and do
Will help to guide my way.

One thing I know for sure
In a world that seems a zoo,
The blessings in the seeds you plant
Will surely come back to you.

The Way It Is

You think you know my business.
Just how can you judge?
I'm fine with being me;
I'm just not going to budge.

It's all so complicated,
And no one knows my biz.
I'll just go ahead and tell you
That's just the way it is.

There Will Be a Corner

Remember when you're feeling down
And there's no end in sight,
There will be a corner
Where you turn and see a light.

Every day becomes a piece
That will be a part of you.
What you do with it
Creates a brand-new you.

Time for Growing

Just when I thought I knew it all
And life was such a bore,
Life decided to teach me things
I'd never known before.

At first I didn't like the change;
I wanted to be the same.
Someone had changed all the rules,
And I didn't know the game.

This experience has really helped me
In ways I'd never known.
But I'd like to keep on growing
Without actually being grown.

To say that you are grown up
Implies that you are done.
Life would be so boring;
It just wouldn't be as fun.

As long as I keep an open mind
Because I never know,
Just when I think I know it all,
It might be time to grow.

Time Is Passing By

So many years.
So many sighs.
So many times
I did not cry.

I know it isn't fair.
I hurt for what is right.
But I can say, "I know
Faith can help me through the night."

Though I may never know
All the reasons why
Life wraps itself around
As time is passing by.

To Be Me

I can't say
What I want to be.
All I want
Is to be me.

I don't want to be famous.
I don't want to be rich.
I know I'd be happy
Just to find my niche.

It's great to laugh.
It's okay to cry.
I'm not hung up
On asking why.

Day by day
And mile by mile,
Just being me
Is my style.

To Be Young Again

You just couldn't pay me
To be young again,
To feel that hurt
Of who I was back then.

I didn't know where I'd end up,
But I kept pushing through,
Determined that my dreams
Would soon be coming true.

My dreams have been adjusted
As time keeps going by.
I'm glad how things turned out,
And I don't question why.

You just couldn't pay me
To be young again,
The angst of reliving
What has already been.

Today's Memory

No matter what I'm doing today,
It's never quite enough.
I want to be somewhere else,
Doing bigger and better stuff.

Why can't I just be happy
Exactly where I am,
And count it as a blessing
That I'm not in a jam?

But when I've made some progress,
And I look at where I've been,
I realize I passed it by
When I play, Remember when?

So no matter where I am
Or how boring life can be,
Today will always be precious
Because I'm making a memory.

Up to Me

As life goes on I know
Sometimes I'll have the blues.
Every life's a winner;
It's up to me to choose.

We Care

I want to touch you
Because I care.
You can't see love,
But it's everywhere.

You're not alone.
If it feels that way,
We're all hoping
And we all pray.

I believe
Our hearts are one,
Our hope is the same
When the day is done.

Keep on going.
You're almost there.
Someone is watching
Because they care.

We Don't Know

Maybe we don't know
All we think we do.
We shrug and keep on going,
I know that I do that too.

We need to keep in mind
When we are making plans,
The future is not guaranteed
And not always in our hands.

It's easy to come crying
For things that are not fair.
Nobody promised easy;
There are hardships everywhere.

There will be blessings
In what you did not get.
And there will be surprises
In what hasn't happened yet.

What I Know

I don't have to know
Each and every thing.
I don't have to know
What each day will bring.

Everything will change
With every brand-new start,
And I will be living
From the bottom of my heart.

What If?

I always wondered, *What if?*
In a worrying kind of way.
I want to be prepared
In case things go astray.

I try to keep in mind
If it doesn't go my way,
That by thinking what if,
I will miss out on today.

Where I'm At

My life is not
The same as yours.
I have windows;
You have doors.

Life doesn't work
If you compare.
The best of life
Is everywhere.

I wouldn't want
To wear your hat.
I want to be
Just where I'm at.

Why?

I shouldn't have done that.
What can I say?
I was definitely wrong
To be acting that way.

I can't change it now,
But I feel the guilt.
I'm sure it would change
Where I am, what I've built.

I like me now.
I hope you're there too.
You were meant to be
Exactly you.

"No regrets,"
Is easy to say.
I wish this guilt
Would go away.

God, he doesn't explain,
So I don't know.
And it's hard to accept
That he wanted it so.

Worry Has Its Limits

I wonder what tomorrow will bring,
If it will be good, maybe bad,
And if what I have today
Is the best that's to be had.

I worry about the weather.
Maybe it will snow.
The money might run out.
Then where will I go?

What if there comes a time
When no one cares about me?
Where will I go, what will I do,
And who is it that I'll be?

But worry is human nature,
And humanity endures.
But someone help me quick.
I've started to budget for my dentures.

You Choose

Who do you want to be?
Where do you want to go?
Did someone promise you
A life without a hoe?

Life is full of surprises,
With onions that make you cry.
Life is how you take it.
Hold your head up as you try.

Giving up is losing,
With sorry, pity as the end.
Create your own future
As a garden you can tend.

You Do You

Judgment has its place,
But how can you know
The choice that others make
From you would be a no?

How boring life would be
Without a choice of what we do.
How about if I do me
And then you can do you?

You Don't Know

I know what I think,
And, of course, I know I'm right.
But I see what you're doing
Shouldn't even see the light.

How can you think I'm wrong
It's so obvious to me?
I know what is best,
And it's the only way to be.

It's never quite that simple,
And it just goes to show
It's so easy to judge
What you really do not know.

You Know

I wanted to write you a love song,
But nothing was good enough.
Everything I tried
Was just silly, fluffy stuff.

If words don't do it justice
Because they never flow,
I'll just hold you close,
Hoping somehow that you know.

Your Heart

It's not your fault
I went away,
No matter what
Your heart might say.

I thought I loved you,
And I wanted to.
You made me happy,
But it wasn't true.

1 went away,
And I hurt you so.
It wasn't right,
But you had to know.

It hurt me too,
To go away.
No matter what
Your heart might say.

Your Voice

You have a voice,
No matter how small.
You can move mountains,
No matter how tall.

We all matter.
We all have a voice.
We can make a difference.
We have that choice.

149

Annual Christmas
Card Poems

2019

From our house to yours,
We're sending you love
As you celebrate
The Son from above.

May you have peace and joy
With plenty of rest.
We're wishing things
That you love the best.

Merry Christmas to all,
With no Grinch to be seen,
May you have special blessings
In 2019.

A Christmas Wish

Christmas is for children
And those young at heart.
A time for gifts, treats, and love,
Where memories get their start.

Here's wishing you a Christmas,
To those both young and old,
A Christmas filled with moments
That will someday turn to gold.

A Christmas We Share

The shopping and lights,
The faces we see
Bring warmth and love
With a Christmas tree.

The gifts we give
With love and care
Bring hope and smiles
For the times we share.

We wish you a Christmas
Filled with good cheer.
We wish you a year
You will always hold dear.

A Lovely Christmas

We wish you a merry Christmas,
One filled with songs we all know.
May all the love and magic
Meet you under the mistletoe.

The twinkling lights upon the tree,
With the angel high above,
Make our hearts so carefree
And warm our days with love.

We wish you a merry Christmas,
Along with a special feast,
And hope the year ahead
Will bring you warmth and peace.

All of Christmas

Christmas is for children.
Are you kidding me?
Christmas is for everyone,
As it was meant to be.

The blessings of Christmas
Are not under the tree.
Love and hope and peace
Are entirely free.

Of course we love the gifts,
But please help us to see
The meaning of those gifts
God gave to you and me.

The songs, the treats, the lights
Are fun this time of year.
We feel a special love
Because the season is here.

The blessings of Christmas—
Joy and hope and peace—
We hope the year ahead
Will be including all of these.

Blessings

Christmas is coming.
Don't forget the mistletoe.
As long as it's cold outside,
I'm hoping it will snow.

Shopping will be special
As we go from store to store.
Don't forget to add your share
To the kettle by the door.

When all the gifts are opened
And we've eaten the table bare,
May the blessings of the season
Find your heart and settle there.

Christmas Cheer

The month of December
Is a favorite time of year,
With an air of warmth and sparkle
As special people gather near.

The years have changed the seasons,
And time has gone by.
Memories warm the heart
As we just smile and sigh.

From our house to yours,
Now that Christmas is near,
We wish you peace and joy
For all the coming year.

Christmas Every Day

Another Christmas,
Another year,
Another chance
For love is here.

The baby boy from up above
Came with a brilliant star,
Bringing all the blessings
No matter where we are.

The gifts that we are given
From those whom we hold dear
Are tokens of love
At this favorite time of year.

We hope you feel the love
We are sending your way.
And that the year ahead
Will be like Christmas every day.

Christmas Far Away

Another Christmas season
Filled with hope and love sincere.
A time that we all treasure
Because love will happen here.

Along with all the presents
And scrumptious things to eat,
We hope that you know
Church is saving you a seat.

We send you all good tidings,
Though we are far away,
And hope you always know
We love you more than we can say.

Christmas Is Everywhere

Christmas is warm and fuzzy,
The best time of the year.
When those who mean the most to us
Will all be gathered near.

As this special day approaches
And we busily prepare,
We shop, bake, and decorate,
And Christmas is everywhere.

May you have a blessed Christmas,
The best that you could know.
And may it wrap around you
Wherever you may go.

Christmas Is for People

Christmas is for people,
No matter who you are.
Everyone's included
Because of a special star.

Always share a smile
With everyone you see.
Send it from the heart
As it was meant to be.

Enjoy the celebration
With lights and gifts galore.
Keep that special feeling
When you come home from the store.

Merry Christmas to you.
May it be warm and kind,
And the year ahead
Be what you had in mind.

Christmas Is Love

We all love Christmas.
That includes me too.
Everything sparkles
In all that we do.

The treats, the songs,
And mistletoe
Give us times
To set our hearts aglow.

We all love Christmas,
Sent from above.
We all need Christmas
Because it's love.

Christmas Love

The treats are baked.
The house is decked.
By now the budget
Is surely wrecked.

The backyard project
Has a ways to go.
But times are busy
As we well know.

School is fine,
With tests all done.
So now it's Christmas
And time for fun.

Here's to Christmas in your heart.
May the child in you always glow.
Here's hoping that the love we send
Will reach your heart and grow.

Heart of Christmas

When I think of Christmas,
It's a time to be kind,
When we leave all things selfish
Far, far behind.

The lights, the tree,
With good things to eat,
With the warmth and joy
That cannot be beat.

This season we love
Is only the start.
The love that we give
Is the season of the heart.

Remember the reason
That comes with joy.
God gave us this season
With a special boy.

Here Comes Christmas

Here comes Christmas,
Here comes love,
Just for us
From a star above.

We've added temptations
Not meant to be.
But it feels so good
If we'd only see.

Peace and joy
Are so much more
Than all the trappings
From all the stores.

We're wishing you joy.
We're wishing you peace.
May all blessings be yours
All years without cease.

Holiday Spirit

Christmas is that time of year
We all love so very much.
When everything around us
Has that special magic touch.

May the warmth and caring in our hearts
As we enjoy the holiday feast
Be only the beginning
As we hope and pray for peace.

And if those Christmas songs
Stay in our hearts to hear,
The sparkle and the spirit
Will keep us through the year.

Merry Christmas one and all.
As your holiday spirits soar,
May it wrap itself around you
And last forevermore.

In Love with Christmas

I've fallen in love with Christmas.
A most wonderful time of year,
When people are sharing love
And spreading holiday cheer.

There are mistletoe and secret gifts,
And love is in the air.
The world's a warm and happy place,
Where people show they care.

Of course it wouldn't be Christmas
Without special things to eat.
And the tradition of years gone by
That comes with your special treat.

There's a special place in your heart
For yesterday's Christmas song.
So sad we can't keep the spirit
Of this season all year long.

Jesus Deep Inside

Another Christmas,
Maybe some snow,
A time to hope
That peace will grow.

A babe so small,
And innocent too,
Came to save us
With love so true.

We wish you a special Christmas,
With love that opens wide.
One that you remember
With Jesus deep inside.

Keep Love and Peace

May the reason for the season
Be on top of your list.
Along with mistletoe
Where we're to be kissed.

May the gifts you give
Be loving and kind,
And the ones you receive
Leave a smile behind.

So eat the treats
And sing a song.
Keep love and peace
All year long.

Reason for the Season

The reason for the season
Is a precious baby boy.
One who gave us love,
Peace and hope and joy.

The message is there
For all to show goodwill,
Not just for Christmastime,
But for all your days to fill.

As you shop for Christmas Day
And hear a Christmas song,
May the blessings of Christmas
Be with you all year long.

Save the Season

If I could save a season,
Christmas would be it.
The kindness, warmth, and love
Would be a perfect fit.

How much better life would be
If I really could.
We'd all care for everybody,
Like we all know we should.

Across the miles at Christmas,
As we're singing loud and strong,
We are wishing you blessings
For now and all year long.

Scrapbook of Christmas

May your scrapbook of Christmas
Be filled with his love.
One full of blessings
He sent from above.

May peace fill your heart
With love and good cheer.
Wishing you blessings
For all the new year.

Sending You Christmas

From our house to yours,
May the season bring love
As you remember the babe
Who was sent from above.

The memories you make
From year to year,
May they warm your heart
As the season draws near.

But most of all,
We hope and pray
That you feel the love
That we're sending your way.

Thank You, God, for Jesus

Thank you, God, for Jesus,
Your one and only Son,
Who paid the price to save us
With our salvation won.

So on this day we celebrate
A special gift of love.
We are so blessed and saved
By our Father from above.

The reason for the season
Is not under the tree.
But why we share our gifts
And the love that came to be.

We hope you feel the joy
As you sing your favorite song.
We pray you keep the spirit
Of this season all year long.

The Christmas We Share

The shopping and lights,
The faces we see
Bring warmth and love
With a Christmas tree.

The gifts we give
With love and care
Bring hope and smiles
For the times we share.

We wish you a Christmas
Filled with good cheer.
We wish you a year
You will always hold dear.

The Magic of Christmas

May the magic of Christmas
Be part of your December.
A season full of moments
That warm your heart when you remember.

May the gifts that you are giving
Be more than you receive.
A time for love and caring
That makes your heart believe.

And when on Christmas morning
You survey the wrapping mess,
We wish the year ahead
Will be one that God will bless.

'Tis the Season

We fell in love with Christmas
So many years ago.
The lights and many presents
Would set our hearts aglow.

The years have changed so many things,
But not the child within.
Christmas is that special time
When we feel like kids again.

So bake your treats, wrap your gifts,
And decorate with flair.
Here's wishing you a season
Filled with love that's everywhere.

Warmth of Christmas

December is my favorite month,
When my heart is warm with love.
The air is filled with laughter
From the mistletoe above.

Everything is lighted
With a special glow.
And everyone smiles at you,
Even those you do not know.

From our house to your house
We send our love to you.
We wish you hope and peace
In a year that's spanking new.

We Give

Shopping for Christmas
On my Surface Pro 3,
Hoping for something special
To put under the tree.

It may seem old fashioned
To think of mistletoe,
But we will be there laughing
For the fun and love we know.

I give to you,
You give to me
As we all smile
With the Christmas tree.

We all know
Because we believe
As we give love,
We will receive.

181

Poems of Faith

God's Point of View

My kind of person
has long been out of style.
But I believe in me,
although I didn't for a while.

I know when times get rough
and the road I cannot see.
When I'm really down and out,
I can always turn to me.

But if I find I'm not that strong
and life is a lethal sword,
I know it's time for a serious talk
as I call upon the Lord.

And when I'm talking with the Lord,
way up in the sky,
somehow he makes me understand,
without ever explaining why.

So when I'm leaving church,
and I'm feeling so brand new,
I realize that God
wanted to share his point of view.

Life can really get me down;
sometimes it looks so bleak.
It's comforting to know
church will be there every week.

Thank You, God

Thank you, God, for giving me
this sunny look at life.
Thank you, God, for helping me
appreciate my strife.
Thank you, God, for giving me
a heart that still can sing.
Thank you, God, for giving me
a gift that's everything.

185

Ending Poem

Each Poem

As time goes on,
We keep hoping,
Wondering if
We can keep on coping.

Each poem I wrote
Is a note to me
So I won't forget
What I need to see.

Maybe a poem
You happened to read
Will come to help,
Like a planted seed.